BLESSINGS OF WEALTH

RESOURCE CREATES RESOURCE

Sheka Mansaray

Revelation Publishing

Kingdom Revelation fit to print

Copyright © 2018 Sheka Mansaray

All rights reserved.

.

All rights reserved. No part of this publication may be reproduced, stored in a retrieval system, or transmitted in any form by any means, electronic, mechanical, photocopy, recording, or otherwise, without the prior permission of the publisher, except as provided by USA copyright law.

Unless otherwise indicated, Scripture quotations are from The Holy Bible, English Standard Version®, copyright © 2001 by Crossway Bibles, a publishing ministry of Revelation publishing. Used by permission. All rights reserved. Scripture quotations marked KJV are from the King James Version of the Bible. Scripture quotations marked NASB are from The New American Standard Bible.® Copyright by permission. Scripture references marked RSV are from The Revised Standard Version. Copyright. All emphases in Scripture quotations have been added by the author. First printing, 2018 Printed in the United States of America.

Table of contents

1. Dollars & cents ...pg 5
2. Resource creates resource ...pg 6
3. True wealth...pg 8
4. Lord giving riches and possessions...pg12
5. Lord causes prosperity ...pg 17
6. Lord gives & Takes away Possessions ...pg 18
7. God owns everything on Earth ...pg 22
8. Financial Health and Prosperity...pg 25
9. Blessings of Wealth ...pg 28
10. Dangers of wealth ...pg 30
11. Poverty Spirit...pg 31
12. Living Out of Poverty...pg 35
13. Promise Prosperity...pg 43
14. Managing Your Finances...pg 47
15. Curses of Witchcraft...pg 64
16. Specific Possessions God owns...pg 72
17. Specific events and items Lord controls ...pg 74
18. Amount to give a tithe...pg 76

Introduction

What does the Bible really say about money? About wealth? How much does God expect you to give to others? How does wealth affect your friendships, marriage, and children? How much is "enough"? The Book "Blessing's of Wealth" is a book that is an essential reading for anyone who is looking to take the Practical Steps mastering the principles with consistency and persistence to transforming Your blessing's into Wealth.

We have come to understand that Many people work hard all their lives save and saving to achieve their dream comprehensive resource for growing, maintaining, and managing wealth across generations. Whether unemployed, underemployed, or still trying to climb the corporate ladder, we're all plagued by money worries and never about the wealth that is promise to us by our maker and father.

We do however come to bear witness to the world and her global prosperous-and-bust economy and documenting its complicated consequences. Within this book you will come to a place where your thoughts will rest in Provoking serious reflection and Revelations, in this book "Blessing's of Wealth" it is not about the rich, however about the desire to be wealthy, at the cost of knowing your father's word and what He already say's about you. Let me not waste any more of yours and mine's time. Let 's excavates in this great work " Blessing's of Wealth"…welcome to you wealth in His word.

DOLLARS AND CENTS

Heaven's economy

Whoever oppresses the poor to increase his own wealth, or gives to the rich, will only come to poverty. Proverbs 22:16

For which of you, desiring to build a tower, does not first sit down and count the cost, whether he has enough to complete it? Luke 14:28

I will bring them back from captivity and return them to Upper Egypt, the land of their ancestry. There they will be a lowly kingdom. Ezekiel 29:14

On that day the Lord will extend His hand a second time to recover the remnant of His people from Assyria, from Egypt, from Pathros, from Cush, from Elam, from Shinar, from Hamath, and from the islands of the sea. Isaiah 11:11

A key to Heaven's economy is to have resources and money. The world is looking for the people who hold these keys to answer big questions and help with huge problems. Finances are an accelerant to solving problems. As a matter of fact, this is the primary way that the western world solves its problems: by throwing money or resources at them. We know that most problems are a lack of relationship, so what happens when we use relationship + resources to solve the problem? We get a solution grounded in permanence. the ability to influence through compassion using your resources and gifts to touch the world. Helping of college scholarships or helping the def with hearing aids, Gifts in Kind including eyeglasses, food items other than protein, Tshirts, DVDs, batteries, stadium seats, refreshments, and dental supplies. The truth is the love for the kids or elders in your hearts motivate you. the world is asking for that love to be proven. Finances and resources help us to father the world back into God's heart.

RESOURCE CREATES RESOURCE

With all my resources I have provided for the temple of my God--gold for the gold work, silver for the silver, bronze for the bronze, iron for the iron and wood for the wood, as well as onyx for the settings, turquoise, stones of various colors, and all kinds of fine stone and marble--all of these in large quantities 1 Chronicles 29:2

Do I have any power to help myself, now that success has been driven from me? Job 6:13
Is my strength like that of stone, or my flesh made of bronze? Job 6:12

"How you have helped the powerless and saved the arm that is feeble! Job 26:2

How you have counseled the unwise and provided fully sound insight! Job 26:3

It takes money to make money.

Resources creates resources and finances create finance. It sounds so simple, but one of the ways we hold this key is create resources and finance in our lifetime and try to multiply them. Many Christians only make enough to last their lifetime, so they aren't thinking of risking, investing, multiplying, and leaving a real inheritance. Some of this comes from bad theology—every Christian generation thinks it's the last, so we don't live for our children's children. It is time to live as though we will be here forever but hope that Jesus will return tomorrow. This will create an incentive, both ways, to be faithful with the resources God has given us for this world and for Jesus. It's not how much money you make but how much money you keep, how hard it works for you, and how many generations you keep it for.

The world around is us is waiting for people who have the resources and connections to finance growth. Producing the resources that solve society's huge problems, or using your finances to build huge futures for cities, is how we will disciple the nations. God really need people who can create community, who can be a resource rather than a requester of it. We need people who the city can look up to in business, education, and media—people who share their lives, resources, and time to make this city great. If we had that, we would be the greatest city on the earth.

True wealth

So if you have not been trustworthy in handling worldly wealth, who will trust you with true riches? Luke 16:11

No one can serve two masters: Either he will hate the one and love the other, or he will be devoted to the one and despise the other. You cannot serve both God and money. Matthew 6:24

I tell you, use worldly wealth to make friends for yourselves, so that when it is gone, they will welcome you into eternal dwellings. Luke 16:9

And if you have not been faithful with the belongings of another, who will give you belongings of your own? Luke 16:12

If you are not doing good with what little you have, depend upon it the more money you got the more selfish you would become, and all the good you appeared to do with your money, if you attempted to do any, would be so much insinuating self-laudation. If your real desire is to do good, there is no need to wait for money before you do it; you can do it now, this very moment, and just where you are. If you are really so unselfish as you believe yourself to be, you will show it by sacrificing yourself for others now. No matter how poor you are, there is room for self-sacrifice, for did not the widow put her all into the treasury? The heart that truly desires to do good does not wait for money before doing it, but comes to the altar of sacrifice and, leaving there the unworthy elements of self, goes out and breathes upon neighbor and stranger, friend and enemy alike the breath of blessedness.

As the effect is related to the cause, so is prosperity and power related to the inward good and poverty and weakness to the inward evil. Money does not constitute true wealth, nor position, nor power, and to rely upon it alone is to stand upon a slippery place. Your true wealth is your stock of virtue, and your true power the uses to which you put it. Rectify your heart, and you will rectify your life. Lust, hatred, anger, vanity, pride, covetousness, self-indulgence, self-seeking, obstinacy,- all these are poverty and weakness; whereas love, purity, gentleness, meekness, compassion, generosity, self-forgetfulness, and self-renunciation,- all these are wealth and power.

As the elements of poverty and weakness are overcome, an irresistible and all-conquering power is evolved from within, and he who succeeds in establishing himself in the highest virtue, brings the whole world to his feet. But the rich, as well as the poor, have their undesirable conditions, and are frequently farther removed from happiness than the poor. And here we see how happiness depends, not upon outward aids or possessions, but upon the inward life. Perhaps you are an employer, and you have endless trouble with those whom you employ, and when you do get good and faithful servants they quickly leave you. As a result you are beginning to lose, or have completely lost, your faith in human nature. You try to remedy matters by giving better wages, and by allowing certain liberties, yet matters remain unaltered. Let me advise you. The secret of all your trouble is not in your servants, it is in yourself; and if you look within, with a humble and sincere desire to discover and eradicate your error, you will, sooner or later, find the origin of all your unhappiness.

It may be some selfish desire, or lurking suspicion, or unkind attitude of mind which sends out its poison upon those about you, and reacts upon yourself, even though you may not show it in your manner or speech. Think of your servants with kindness, consider of them that extremity of service which you yourself would not care to perform were you in their place. Rare and beautiful is that humility of soul by which a servant entirely forgets himself in his master's good; but far rarer, and beautiful with a divine beauty, is that nobility of soul by which a man, forgetting his own happiness, seeks the happiness of those who are under his authority, and who depend upon him for their bodily sustenance. And such a man's happiness is increased tenfold, nor does he need to complain of those whom he employs. Said a well known and extensive employer of labor, who never needs to dismiss an employee: "I have always had the happiest relations with my workpeople.

If you ask me how it is to be accounted for, I can only say that it has been my aim from the first to do to them as I would wish to be done by." Herein lies the secret by which all desirable conditions are secured, and all that are undesirable are overcome. Do you say that you are lonely and unloved, and have "not a friend in the world"? Then, I pray you, for the sake of your own happiness, blame nobody but yourself. Be friendly towards others, and friends will soon flock round you. Make yourself pure and lovable, and you will be loved by all.

Whatever conditions are rendering your life burdensome, you may pass out of and beyond them by developing and utilizing within you the transforming power of self-purification and self-conquest. Be it the poverty which galls (and remember that the poverty upon which I have been dilating is that poverty which is a source of misery, and not that voluntary poverty which is the glory of emancipated souls), or the riches which burden, or the many misfortunes, griefs, and annoyances which form the dark background in the web of life, you may overcome them by overcoming the selfish elements within which give them life.

It matters not that by the unfailing Law, there are past thoughts and acts to work out and to atone for, as, by the same law, we are setting in motion, during every moment of our life, fresh thoughts and acts, and we have the power to make them good or ill. Nor does it follow that if a man (reaping what he has sown) must lose money or forfeit position, that he must also lose his fortitude or forfeit his uprightness, and it is in these that his wealth and power and happiness are to be found. He who clings to self is his own enemy and is surrounded by enemies. He who relinquishes self is his own savior, and is surrounded by friends like a protecting belt. Before the divine radiance of a pure heart all darkness vanishes and all clouds melt away, and he who has conquered self has conquered the universe.

Come, then, out of your poverty; come out of your pain; come out of your troubles, and sighings, and complainings, and heartaches, and loneliness by coming out of yourself. Let the old tattered garment of your petty selfishness fall from you, and put on the new garment of universal Love. You will then realize the inward heaven, and it will be reflected in all your outward life. He who sets his foot firmly upon the path of self-conquest, who walks, aided by the staff of Faith, the highway of self-sacrifice, will assuredly achieve the highest prosperity, and will reap abounding and enduring joy and bliss. To them that seek the highest good All things subserve the wisest ends; Nothing comes as ill, and wisdom lends Wings to all shapes of evil offspring. The darkening sorrow veils a Star That waits to shine with gladsome light; Hell waits on heaven; and after night Comes golden glory from afar. Defeats are steps by which we climb with purer aim to nobler ends; Loss leads to gain, and joy attends True footsteps up the hills of time. Pain leads to paths of holy bliss, To thoughts and words and deeds divine-, And clouds that gloom and rays that shine, Along life's upward highway kiss.

Misfortune does but cloud the way Whose end and summit in the sky Of bright success, sunrises' and high, Awaits our seeking and our stay. The heavy pall of doubts and fears That clouds the Valley of our hopes, The shades with which the spirit copes, The bitter harvesting of tears, The heartaches, miseries, and griefs, The bruisings born of broken ties, All these are steps by which we rise To living ways of sound beliefs. Love, pitying, watchful, runs to meet The Pilgrim from the Land of Fate; All glory and all good await The coming of obedient feet.

Lord giving riches and possessions

He will no longer be rich and his wealth will not endure, nor will his possessions spread over the land. Job 15:29

They sold property and possessions to give to anyone who had need. Acts 2:45

Jesus told him, "If you want to be perfect, go, sell your possessions and give to the poor, and you will have treasure in heaven. Then come, follow Me." Matthew 19:21

There were no needy ones among them, because those who owned lands or houses would sell their property, bring the proceeds from the sales, Acts 4:34

1.   Examples of Lord giving riches and possessions

Lord gave children of Israel the promised land "The land which I [the Lord] gave to Abraham and Isaac, I will give it to you, and I will give the land to your descendants after you" (Genesis 35:12).

I will bring you to the land which I swore to give to Abraham, Isaac, and Jacob, and I will give it to you for a possession; I am the Lord (Exodus 6:8).

I am the Lord your God, who brought you out of the land of Egypt to give you the land of Canaan and to be your God (Leviticus 25:38). Then it shall come about when the Lord your God brings you into the land which He swore to your fathers, Abraham, Isaac and Jacob, to give you, great and splendid cities which you did not build, and houses full of all good things which you did not fill, and hewn cisterns which you did not dig, vineyards and olive trees which you did not plant, and you shall eat and be satisfied, then watch yourself, lest you forget the Lord (Deuteronomy 6:10-12). For the Lord your God is bringing you into a good land, a land of brooks of water, of fountains and springs, flowing forth in valleys and hills; a land of wheat and barley, of vines and fig trees and pomegranates, a land of olive oil and honey; a land where you shall eat food without scarcity, in which you shall not lack anything; a land whose stones are iron, and out of whose hills you can dig copper.

When you have eaten and are satisfied, you shall bless the Lord your God for the good land which He has given you (Deuteronomy 8:7-10). Then it shall be, when you enter the land which the Lord your God gives you as an inheritance, and you possess it and live in it, that you shall take some of the first of all the ground which you shall bring in from your land that the Lord your God gives you...you shall go to the priest who is in office at that time, and say to him, 'I declare this day to the Lord my God that I have entered the land which the Lord swore to our fathers to give us' (Deuteronomy 26:1-3) I [the Lord] gave you a land on which you had not labored, and cities which you had not built, and you have lived in them; and you are eating of vineyards and oliveyards which you did not plant (Joshua 24:13). You told them to enter in order to possess the land which You swore to give them (Nehemiah 9:15).

Behold we are slaves today, and as to the land which You did give to our fathers to eat of its fruit and its boundary, behold, we are slaves on it (Nehemiah 9:36). For if you truly amend your ways and your deeds, if you truly practice justice...then I will let you dwell in this place, in the land that I gave to your fathers forever (Jeremiah 7:5-7).

Other examples The Lord has greatly blessed my master [Abraham], so that he has become rich; and He has given him flocks and herds, and silver and gold, and servants and maids, and camels and donkeys (Genesis 24:35). Now Isaac sowed in that land, and reaped in the same year a hundredfold. And the Lord blessed him, and the man became rich, and continued to grow richer until he became very wealthy; for he had possessions of flocks and herds and a great household (Genesis 26:12-14). The Lord your God will bring you into the land which your fathers possessed, and you shall possess it; and He will prosper you and multiply you more than your fathers (Deuteronomy 30:5). David was prospering in all his ways for the Lord was with him (1 Samuel 18:14-15).

Now it was told King David, saying, "The Lord has blessed the house of Obed-edom and all that belongs to him, on account of the ark of God (2 Samuel 6:12). God said to Solomon... I will give you riches and wealth and honor, such as none of the kings who were before you has possessed, nor those who will come after you" (2 Chronicles 1:11-12). He hired also 100,000 valiant warriors out of Israel for one hundred talents of silver. But a man of God came to him saying, "O king, do not let the army of Israel go with you... Amaziah said to the man of God, "But what shall we do for the hundred talents which I have given to the troops And the man of God answered, "The Lord has much more to give you than this" (2 Chronicles 25:6-9).

Then Satan answered the Lord, "Does Job fear God for nothing? Have You not made a hedge about him and his house and all that he has, on every side? You have blessed the work of his hands, and his possessions have increased in the land (Job 1:9-10). The Lord restored the fortunes of Job when he prayed for his friends, and the Lord increased all that Job had twofold...the Lord blessed the latter days of Job more than his beginning, and he had 14,000 sheep, and 6,000 camels, and 1,000 yoke of oxen, and 1,000 female donkeys (Job 42:10,12). He brought them out with silver and gold (Psalm 105:37). I will give you [Cyrus] the treasures of darkness, and hidden wealth of secret places, in order that you may know that it is I, The Lord, the God of Israel, who calls you by your name (Isaiah 45:3).

Now I have given all these lands into the hand of Nebuchadnezzar king of Babylon, My servant (Jeremiah 27:5-7). "Thus you were adorned with gold and silver...your fame went forth among the nations on account of your beauty, for it was perfect because of My splendor which I bestowed on you," declares the Lord God...You also took your beautiful jewels made of My gold and of My silver, which I had given you, and made for yourself male images...Also My bread which I gave you, fine flour, oil, and honey with which I fed you, you would offer before them for a soothing aroma; so it happened," declares the Lord God (Ezekiel 16:13,14,17-19). Nebuchadnezzar king of Babylon made his army labor hard against Tyre; every head was made bald, and every shoulder was rubbed bare. But he and his army had no wages from Tyre for the labor that he had performed against it. Therefore, thus says the Lord God, "Behold, I shall give the land of Egypt to Nebuchadnezzar king of Babylon. And he will carry off her wealth, and capture her spoil and seize her plunder; and it will be wages for his army" (Ezekiel 29:18-19). For she [Israel] does not know that it was I who gave her the grain, the new wine, and the oil, and lavished on her silver and gold, which they used for Baal (Hosea 2:8).

Abraham did not want to give another person credit for his becoming rich Abram said to the king of Sodom, "I have sworn to the Lord God Most High, possessor of heaven and earth, that I will not take a thread or a sandal thong or anything that is yours, lest you should say, 'I have made Abram rich'" (Genesis 14:22-23).

2. Lord sometimes gives riches after testing and humbling He led you through the great and terrible wilderness, with its fiery serpents and scorpions and thirsty ground where there was no water; He brought water for you out of the rock of flint. In the wilderness He fed you manna which your fathers did not know, that He might humble you and that He might test you, to do good for you in the end. Otherwise, you may say in your heart, 'My power and the strength of my hand made me this

wealth.' But you shall remember the Lord your God, for it is He who is giving you power to make wealth (Deuteronomy 8:15-18). For You have tried us, O God; You have refined us as silver is refined. You brought us into the net; You laid an oppressive burden upon our loins. You made men ride over our heads; we went through the fire and water; yet You brought us out into a place of abundance (Psalm 66:10-12).

3. Lord gives possessions to His children even in their sleep He gives to His beloved even in his sleep (Psalm 127:2).

4. When Lord gives riches, it is a blessing It is the blessing of the Lord that makes rich, and He adds no sorrow to it (Proverbs 10:22).

5. Lord giving possessions conditioned upon obedience (See Our Part Scriptures) 6. Lord gives us precisely enough Thus says the Lord God of Israel, 'It is I who anointed you [David] king over Israel... I also gave you your master's house and...I gave you the house of Israel and Judah; and if that had been too little, I would have added to you many more things like these!" (2 Samuel 12:7-8).

• According to our ability to handle possessions For it is just like a man about to go on a journey, who called his own slaves, and entrusted his possessions to them. And to one he gave five talents, to another, two, and to another, one, each according to his own ability (Matthew 25:14-15).

LORD CAUSES PROSPERITY

Jacob said, "O God of my father Abraham and God of my father Isaac, O Lord, who said to me, 'Return to your country and to your relatives, and I will prosper you' (Genesis 32:9).

"For You said, 'I will surely prosper you [Jacob], and make your descendants as the sand of the sea, which cannot be numbered for multitude'" (Genesis 32:12).

The Lord was with Joseph, so he became a successful man. And he was in the house of his master, the Egyptian. Now his master saw that the Lord was with him and how the Lord caused all that he did to prosper in his hand (Genesis 39:2-3).

The chief jailer did not supervise anything under Joseph's charge because the Lord was with him; and whatever he did, the Lord made to prosper (Genesis 39:21-23).

1. Prosperity conditioned upon obedience and seeking the Lord (See Our Part Scriptures)

2. Prayers for Lord to bless financially May the Lord give you increase, you and your children (Psalm 115:14). O Lord, do save, we beseech You; O Lord, we beseech You, do send prosperity! (Psalm 118:25). Beloved, I pray that in all respects you may prosper and be in good health, just as your soul prospers (3 John 2).

LORD GIVES & TAKES AWAY POSSESSIONS

The LORD is a jealous and avenging God; the LORD takes vengeance and is filled with wrath. The LORD takes vengeance on his foes and vents his wrath against his enemies. Nahum 1:2

when I sharpen My flashing sword, and My hand grasps it in judgment, I will take vengeance on My adversaries and repay those who hate Me. Deuteronomy 32:41

He said, "Naked I came from my mother's womb, and naked I shall return there. The Lord gave and the Lord has taken away. Blessed be the name of the Lord." Through all this Job did not sin nor did he blame God (Job 1:21-22).

Then his wife said to him, "Do you still hold fast your integrity? Curse God and die!" But he said to her, "You speak as one of the foolish women speaks. Shall we indeed accept good from God and not accept adversity?" In all this Job did not sin with his lips (Job 2:9-10).

1. Lord makes rich and poor The Lord make poor and rich; he brings low, He also exalts (1 Samuel 2:7). In the day of prosperity be happy, but in the day of adversity consider—God has made the one as well as the other so that man may not discover anything that will be after him (Ecclesiastes 7:14).

2. Lord takes away or withholds possessions when unfaithful, disobedient, or not seeking the Lord (see Our Part Scriptures)

Lord is merciful and will provide a means of restoration So they forsook the Lord and served Baal and the Astarte's. And the anger of the Lord burned against Israel, and He gave them into the hands of plunders who plundered them; and He sold them into the hands of their enemies around them, so that they could no longer stand before their enemies. Wherever they went, the hand of the Lord was against them for evil, as the Lord had spoken and as the Lord had sworn to them, so that they were severely distressed. Then the Lord raised up judges who delivered them from the hands of those who plundered them (Judges 2:13-16).

I will restore your fortunes and will gather you from all the nations and from all the places where I have driven you, 'declares the Lord (Jeremiah 29:14). Men shall buy fields for money, sign and seal deeds, and call in witnesses in the land of Benjamin, in the environs of Jerusalem... for I will restore their fortunes declares the Lord (Jeremiah 32:44).

I will restore the fortunes of Judah and the fortunes of Israel, and I will rebuild them as they were at first... I will restore the fortunes of the land as they were at first, says the Lord... I will restore their fortunes and will have mercy on them (Jeremiah 33:7, 11, 26). "Yet I will restore the fortunes of Moab in the latter days," declares the Lord (Jeremiah 48:47). "I will restore the fortunes of the sons of Ammon," declares the Lord (Jeremiah 49:6). For behold, in those days and at that time, when I restore the fortunes of Judah and Jerusalem, I will gather [for judgment] all the nations (Joel 3:1-2). For the Lord their God will care for them [Israel] and restore their fortune (Zephaniah 2:7). "Indeed, I will give you [Israel] renown and praise among all the peoples of the earth, when I restore your fortunes before your eyes," says the Lord (Zephaniah 3:20). 'For before those days [return from captivity] there was no wage for man or wage for animal... But now I will not treat the remnant of this people as in the former days,' declares the Lord of hosts. For there will be peace for the seed: the vine will yield its fruit, the land will yield its produce, and the heavens will give their dew; and I will cause the remnant of this people to inherit all these things (Zechariah 8:10-12).

3. Lord takes away wealth of ungodly people and nations The Lord will tear down the house of the proud, but He will establish the boundary of the widow (Proverbs 15:25). I will make a spoil of your [Tyre] riches and a prey of your merchandise, break down your walls and destroy your pleasant houses... I will make you a bear rock; you will be a place for the spreading of nets. You will be built no more, for I the Lord have spoken (Ezekiel 26:12, 14).

For Tyre built herself a fortress and piled up silver like dust, and gold like the mire of the streets. Behold, the Lord will dispossess her and cast her wealth into the sea; and she will be consumed with fire (Zechariah 9:3-4). Behold, a day is coming for the Lord when the spoil taken from you will be divided among you. For I will gather all the nations against Jerusalem to battle, and the city will be captured, the houses plundered (Zechariah 14:1-2).

4. Lord sometimes transfers wealth from ungodly to godly You know that I [Jacob] served your father with all my strength. Yet your father has cheated me and changed my wages ten times; however, God did not allow him to hurt me... Thus God has taken away your father's livestock and given them to me (Genesis 31:6-7, 9). Rachel and Leah answered and said to him, "Do we still have any portion or inheritance in our father's house? Are we not reckoned by him as foreigners? For he has sold us, and has also entirely consumed our purchase price. Surely all the wealth which God has taken from our father belongs to us and our children (Genesis 31:14-16).

LORD PROTECTS OUR POSSESSIONS

Then Satan answered the Lord, "Does Job fear God for nothing? Have You not made a hedge about him and his house and all that he has, on every side? You have blessed the work of his hands, and his possessions have increased in the land (Job 1:9-10). If the God of my father, the God of Abraham, and the fear of Isaac, had not been for me [Jacob], surely now you [Laban] would have sent me away empty-handed. God has seen my affliction and the toil of my hands, so He rendered judgment last night (Genesis 31:42).

GOD OWNS EVERYTHING ON EARTH

GOD OWNS EVERYTHING ON EARTH He [Melchizedek] blessed him and said, "Blessed be Abram of God Most High, possessor of heaven and earth" (Genesis 14:19)

Abram said to the king of Sodom, "I have sworn to the Lord God Most High, possessor of heaven and earth (Genesis 14:22).

Moses said to him [Pharaoh], "As soon as I go out of the city, I will spread out my hands to the Lord; the thunder will cease, and there will be hail no longer, that you may know that the earth is the Lord's" (Exodus 9:29).

Now then, if you will indeed obey My voice and keep My covenant, then you shall be My own possession among all the peoples, for all the earth is Mine (Exodus 19:5).

Behold, to the Lord your God belong heaven and the highest heavens, the earth and all that is in it (Deuteronomy 10:14).

Your, O Lord, is... everything that is in the heavens and the earth... who am I and who are my people that we should be able to offer as generously as this? For all things come from You, and from Your hand we have given You. For we are sojourners before You, and tenants... all this abundance that we have provided to build You a house for Your holy name, it is from Your hand, and all is Yours (1 Chronicles 29:11,14-16).

Who has given to Me that I should repay him? Whatever is under the whole heaven is Mine (Job 41:11).

The earth is the Lord's, and all it contains, the world, and those who dwell in it (Psalm 24:1). If I were hungry, I would not tell you; for the whole world is Mine; and all it contains (Psalm 50:12).

Arise, O God, judge the earth! For it is Thou does possess all the nations (Psalm 82:8). The heavens are Yours, the earth also is Yours; the world and all it contains, You have founded them (Psalm 89:11). In whose hands are the depths of the earth; the peaks of the mountains are His also. The sea is His, for it was He who made it; and His hands formed the dry land (Psalm 95:4-5).

O Lord, how many are Your works! In wisdom You have made them all; the earth if full of Your possessions (Psalm 104:24).

For the earth is the Lord's, and everything that is in it (1 Corinthians 10:26).

1. Parable illustrating God's ownership For it is just like a man about to go on a journey, who called his own slaves, and entrusted his possessions to them. And to one he gave five talents, to another, two, and to another, one, each according to his own ability; and he went on his journey. Immediately the one who had received the five talents went and traded with them, and gained five more talents. In the same manner the one who had received the two talents gained two more. But he who received the one talent went away and dug in the ground, and hid his master's money.

Now after a long time, the master of those slaves came and settled accounts with them. And the one who had received the five talents came up and brought five more talents, saying, 'Master, you entrusted five talents to me; see, I have gained five more talents.' His master said to him, 'Well done, good and faithful slave; you were faithful with a few things, I will put you in charge of many things, enter into the joy of your master.' The one also who had received the two talents came up and said, 'Master, you entrusted to me two talents; see, I have gained two more talents.' His master said to him, 'Well done, good and faithful slave; you were faithful with a few things, I will put you in charge of many things; enter into the joy of your master.' And the one also who had received the one talent came up and said, 'Master, I knew you to be a hard man, reaping where you did not sow, and gathering where you scattered no seed. And I was afraid, and went away and hid your talent in the ground; see, you have what is yours.' But his master answered and said to him, 'You wicked, lazy slave, you knew that I reap where I did not sow, and gather where I scattered no seed. Then you ought to have put my money in the bank, and on my arrival I would have received my money back with interest. Therefore take away the talent from him, and give it to the one who has ten talents' (Matthew 25:14-28).

2. Lord holds all things together He... upholds all things by the word of His power (Hebrews 1:3). In Him all things hold together (Colossians 1:17).

Financial Health and Prosperity

Whoever can be trusted with very little can also be trusted with much, and whoever is dishonest with very little will also be dishonest with much Luke 16:10

His master replied, 'Well done, good and faithful servant! You have been faithful with a few things; I will put you in charge of many things. Enter into the joy of your master!' Matthew 25:21

His master replied, 'Well done, good servant! Because you have been faithful in a very small matter, you shall have authority over ten cities.' Luke 19:17

and said, "I swear by myself, declares the LORD, that because you have done this and have not withheld your son, your only son, I will surely bless you and make your descendants as numerous as the stars in the sky and as the sand on the seashore. Your descendants will take possession of the cities of their enemies, Genesis 22:16-17

1. With privilege comes responsibility . You'll never manage a million dollars correctly if you can't handle $10. The same mindset that causes $10 to slip through your fingers will cause a million to slip away just as easily.

2. I used to tell myself there's more where that came from. That horrible thought makes me want to cry. I disrespected my salary. I dismissed the hard work and skill that helped me earn that salary.

How many times have you said, it's just $1. It's just $10. That's not much. Maybe it's not. But you are not looking at the power of what is in your hands. There are wonderful dollar stores in the city where I live. You can buy $1 items online too.

I look at my finances completely different now. I don't tell myself I just have anything. It ALL has value. I once saved up my spare change for a whole year. During the Christmas season, I was able to pay for my dinner at an expensive restaurant.

3. I came to understand that what I desired more than anything was to be closer to God. I wanted to love myself and have others in my life that loved me. I wanted to discover who God made me to be. This is one of the most vital keys of all. You will never enjoy money without having these true riches in your life first. They are so much greater than money.

4. Yes, your Heavenly Father is rich and can drop a ton of cash on you in an instant. He is also a wise and responsible parent. He doesn't always give you what you want when you want it if it's not best for you. God is more interested in your loving Him above all else. Can you say this is true for your life? He wants to develop His character in you by removing harmful flaws from your soul. Do you have an open heart to let Him do this work?

5. When you're in the valley, you know you need God. But when things are going well, it's easy to trust in material blessings. However, doing so creates a false sense of security.

In Deuteronomy Chapter 8, the Lord warned the Israelites not to forget Him. He was about to bring them into a huge place of prosperity and He wanted to make sure they remembered He was the one who made that prosperity possible.

6. God does not pour out provision just so you can have everything you want. He wants you to be generous and help someone else.

7. including the 90 percent left over after you tithe. Put it ALL in God's hands.

8. God's wisdom brings lasting wealth . Read that again. Chasing after money doesn't bring lasting wealth but going after God's wisdom will! Many people prosper in this world without God's help. But a lot of them are miserable and lonely. Also, keep in mind that wealth does not include money only. It also includes the people in your life that love you and most of all your relationship with God. When King Soloman took the throne, the Lord asked him what he wanted most. He chose wisdom. Because of that, the Lord blessed him with great riches as well.

Discovery our purpose and sell out to what   you are designed to

 be and do in this earth . When I look at the lives of the godly men and women who are experiencing success, I see they have answered the call of God and have dedicated themselves to fulfilling their purpose. There is one word that sums all this up and that is obedience. Isaiah 1:19 says that when you are willing and obedient, you will eat the good of the land.

9. The Missing Bible Secret about Financial Health & Prosperity…

Beloved, God wants you to experience great financial prosperity so that you can show the world you have a Heavenly Father who cherishes His children. But He also wants you to think of others who are in need. But first, you must learn to treasure what you already have. You must allow the Bible to govern every aspect of your life

BLESSINGS OF WEALTH

The blessing of the Lord, it maketh rich, and he addeth no sorrow with it. Proverbs 10:22

And God is able to bless you abundantly, so that in all things at all times, having all that you need, you will abound in every good work. 2 Corinthians 9:8

1 Blessed is the one who does not walk in step with the wicked or stand in the way that sinners take or sit in the company of mockers, 2 but whose delight is in the law of the LORD, and who meditates on his law day and night. 3 That person is like a tree planted by streams of water, which yields its fruit in season and whose leaf does not wither— whatever they do prospers. Psalm 1:1-3

1. Godly rich people

28 May God give you heaven's dew and earth's richness— an abundance of grain and new wine.

29 May nations serve you and peoples bow down to you. Be lord over your brothers, and may the sons of your mother bow down to you. May those who curse you be cursed and those who bless you be blessed." Genesis 27:28-29

A. RIGHTEOUS WILL BE REWARDED WITH PROSPERITY

B. WEALTH FOR THOSE WHO MEDITATE ON WORD

C. THE PROSPEROUS WILL WORSHIP THE LORD

D. PRAYING FOR PROSPERITY

    2. Things that keep one from wealth

16 and said, "I swear by myself, declares the LORD, that because you have done this and have not withheld your son, your only son,
17 I will surely bless you and make your descendants as numerous as the stars in the sky and as the sand on the seashore. Your descendants will take possession of the cities of their enemies, Genesis 22:16-17

E. LORD DELIGHTS IN PROSPERITY OF HIS SERVANT

F. NOT ALL WILL PROSPER

    3. JESUS WORTHY TO RECEIVE RICHES

Jesus has been found worthy of greater honor than Moses, just as the builder of a house has greater honor than the house itself. Hebrews 3:3

H. THE WISE WILL BECOME RICH

I. HOW WEALTH IS ACQUIRED

DANGERS OF WEALTH

DANGERS OF WEALTH

And every house is built by someone, but God is the builder of everything. Hebrews 3:4

A. LOVING WEALTH

B. RICHES PRODUCE PRIDE

    1. Should not be proud because life is short

    2. Boast in Lord not riches

C. RICHES AFFORD A FALSE SENSE OF SECURITY

    1. Some trust in riches

D. WEALTH TENDS TO SEPARATE PEOPLE

    1. Wealth can separate Christians

E. RICHES ARE DECEITFUL/CAN CHOKE FRUITFULNESS

F. HARD FOR RICH TO ENTER THE KINGDOM OF GOD

    1. Rich who do not know Lord will be eternally separated from Him

G. RICH THINK THEY ARE WISE

H. RICH TREAT POOR UNFAIRLY

I. WHEN WEALTHY WE CAN FORGET GOD

J. WEALTH CREATES ENVY.

Poverty Spirit

For you know the grace of our Lord Jesus Christ, that though he was rich, yet for your sake he became poor, so that you through his poverty might become rich. 2 Corinthians 8:9

Though he was rich: means - wealth (as fulness), that is, (literally) money, possessions, or (figuratively) abundance, richness, (specifically) valuable bestowment: - riches.

Rich: to be (or become) wealthy: - be increased with goods, (be made, wax) rich.

Poor: To become a beggar, indigent, Stingy: Extreme & often niggardly frugality (cheap, cheesy, mean spirited in giving, no generosity) Joh 10:10 The thief comes only in order to steal and kill and destroy. I came that they may have and enjoy life, and have it in abundance (to the full, till it overflows).

THE POVERY SPIRIT

Its main goal is to keep you in lack of everything needed to do God's will. It blocks every move towards the purpose of God. It robs you of God's power, and authority, and kingdom thinking.... It robs you of God's peace, joy, happiness, etc. It sets you up to accept or be comfortable with lack It effects relationships It steals your passion and zeal for God. It brings you into shame, guilt, and reproach It causes oppression, depression, strife, bickering, contentions etc. Its root is in the spirit of python which squeezes the life out of you. It poisons your conversation and confession of faith. (poor mouth) It will cause you to accept and live with an unclean spirit. (dirty house, laziness, procrastination, apathy, passivity, etc.

A POVERTY SPIRIT

is not just about money. People can be rich in things and still live in poverty.

POVERTY IS A SPIRITUAL NATURE OF LACK,

TO DO WITHOUT, TO NOT HAVE, TO BE POOR, DESTITUTE, Num 13:30 And Caleb stilled the people before Moses, and said, Let us go up at once, and possess it; for we are well able to overcome it. 31 But the men that went up with him said, We be not able to go up against the people; for they are stronger than we. Num 13:33 And there we saw the giants, the sons of Anak, which come of the giants: and we were in our own sight as grasshoppers, and so we were in their sight. Not having sufficient resources to live life prescribed according to what Jesus provided to us.

DESTITUTE:

without the things necessary to sustain or have even the menial basics of life. Poverty Curses: (caused by us not being obedient to God and God's ways) – Matt 6:33 Deu 28:15 But it shall come to pass, if thou wilt not hearken unto the voice of the LORD thy God, to observe to do all his commandments and his statutes which I command thee this day; that all these curses shall come upon thee, and overtake thee: The curse of Cain. -- withholding his best offering - cursed in his ability to produce a harvest – wandering the land of Nod with nothing, a fugitive and vagabond – Gen 4:11,12 Pro 3:9 Honor the LORD with thy substance, and with the firstfruits of all thine increase: 10 So shall thy barns be filled with plenty, and thy presses shall burst out with new wine. The curse of Malachi. Malachi 3:10-11 bring the tithes and offerings into the storehouse. God promises to open the windows of heaven and to rebuke the devourer on our behalf.

Many are plagued with curses because they do not honor God in their tithes and offerings. The tithe belongs to God - Lev 27:30 Passivity Oppression Apathy Fear Procrastination Depression Death Doubt Darkness Indifference...The curse of Haggai. The people's disobedience to God produced bad fruit and brought poverty into their lives in several ways. They neglected the house of God. Hag. 1:1 and forward The generational curse of poverty. Exodus 20:5 explains that the iniquities of the fathers can affect as many as four generations. Deuteronomy 28:46 says, "And they shall be upon thee for a sign and for a wonder, and upon thy seed for ever" The curse of Ananias and Sapphira. In a time of great revival, the people were laying their offerings at the feet of the apostles (see Acts 5:34-37). But Ananias and Sapphira withheld from the church a portion of the profits from the sale of their property and lied about it to the Holy Ghost. Both of them received the same punishment--death--when Peter exposed their sin.

IS God's PLAN FOR HIS KIDS TO BE RICH

– YES WITH THE RIGHT MOTIVE – FOR HIS GLORY Abraham: Gen 13:2 Noah: Built an ark – costs a lot of money Solomon: I Kings 10:1-10 – What the right riches bring (fame, favor, happy people, excellence in all areas) I Kings 10:21,27 (silver was much in abundance it was made of no value,as trash, In Chapter 10 -(gold mentioned 44 times in 29 ver.) One years worth of gold – 666 talents of gold - $ 319,680,000 per year of gold only. 1Ki 11:3 And he had seven hundred wives, princesses, and three hundred concubines: and his wives turned away his heart. (talk about expensive shopping trips) Deu 8:18 But thou shalt remember the LORD thy God: for it is he that giveth thee power to get wealth, that he may establish his covenant which he sware unto thy fathers, as it is this day. Psa 66:12 Thou hast caused men to ride over our heads; we went through fire and through water: but thou broughtest us out into a wealthy place. 3Jn 1:2 Beloved, I pray that you may prosper (succeed) in every way and [that your body] may keep well, even as [I know] your soul keeps well and prospers.

Psa 50:10 For every beast of the forest is mine, and the cattle upon a thousand hills. Luk 4:18 The Spirit of the Lord is upon me, because he hath anointed me to preach the gospel to the poor; he hath sent me to heal the brokenhearted, to preach deliverance to the captives, and recovering of sight to the blind, to set at liberty them that are bruised, 19 To preach the acceptable year of the Lord. Psa 23:1 The Lord is my shepherd, I shall not want. Jas 1:4 But let patience have her perfect work, that ye may be perfect and entire, wanting nothing. Php 4:11 Not that I am implying that I was in any personal want, for I have learned how to be content (satisfied to the point where I am not disturbed or disquieted) in whatever state I am.

A GREAT LACK

It is a sin to live below the standard that God set how we should live, in Him. It is a sin to live a powerless life in God being in poverty with the gifts of God that He has bestowed. Many people will fight over a small point of doctrine or custom and yet not even notice the state of a powerless, pathetic, weak, defeated church. This is spiritual poverty at its greatest effect!

POVERTY IS PRIMARILY VISIBLE IN THE MONEY REALM

Through God's power, all these financial curses can be broken. I have seen people with tragic situations miraculously set free. But I get the greatest joy out of seeing a poverty-stricken person transition into the financial promises of God.

LIBERTY FROM LACK

The keys to freedom from poverty are available to every one of us who is willing to do what God tells us in His Word. Then you can reverse the curses mentioned and, with God's help, break their power over your life.

Living Out of Poverty

For you know the grace of our Lord Jesus Christ, that though he was rich, yet for your sake he became poor, so that you through his poverty might become rich. 2 Corinthians 8:9

just as the Son of Man did not come to be served, but to serve, and to give His life as a ransom for many." Matthew 20:28

For even Christ did not please Himself, but as it is written: "The insults of those who insult You have fallen on Me." Romans 15:3

sorrowful, yet always rejoicing; poor, yet making many rich; having nothing, and yet possessing everything. 2 Corinthians 6:10

May the grace of the Lord Jesus Christ, and the love of God, and the fellowship of the Holy Spirit be with all of you. 2 Corinthians 13:14

Who, existing in the form of God, did not consider equality with God something to be grasped, Philippians 2:6

but emptied Himself, taking the form of a servant, being made in human likeness. Philippians 2:7

And being found in appearance as a man, He humbled Himself and became obedient to death--even death on a cross. Philippians 2:8

I know your affliction and your poverty--though you are rich! And I am aware of the slander of those who falsely claim to be Jews, but are in fact a synagogue of Satan. Revelation 2:9

      Healing from the Spirit of Poverty Most of the world lives in poverty. In many countries, it's a way of life which has embedded itself within the culture, and it has remained that way for as many generations as anyone can remember. Poverty permeates the mindsets and the attitudes of the people. Unfortunately, they know no other way. Living in poverty is accepted and expected; it becomes a generational trend within a poverty culture. Regrettably, most Christians do not realize that Jesus' death on the cross provided not only for the forgiveness of our sins and for healing from our sicknesses, but additionally for healing from poverty. Take into consideration the following scriptures: "For ye know the grace of our Lord Jesus Christ, that, though He was rich, for your sakes he became poor, that ye through His poverty might be rich"— 2 Cor. 8:9, and, "Worthy is the Lamb that was slain to [in order that we might] receive power, and riches… and blessing"–Rev. 5:12* One of the biggest limitations to receiving God's abundance in our lives is the lack of understanding and acknowledgment that blessings of prosperity are one of the reasons Jesus died for us on the cross.

We have no problem believing He died for our sins. And many accept as well that He died for our healing (of body, mind and spirit). Why, then, do we have a problem believing He died to free us from a state of poverty? Again, realize that Jesus died for...

(1) our sins (salvation),

(2) our sicknesses (healing of body, mind and spirit), and

(3) our finances (our fiscal needs). . Jesus has paid the price that we might be "rich." Likewise, Jesus' death on the cross atoned for the "curse of poverty." Take notice below of how this fact is revealed in Scripture:

• He hadn't eaten in over 24 hours (Hunger)

• He was thirsty ("I thirst") (Thirst)

• He had nothing and was stripped of his cloak (Nakedness)

• He had no burial place (In need) Unfortunately most Christians do not realize that, as a child of the King and an heir to His promises, we are entitled to the financial blessings afforded us because of the cross. The first step in healing from the curse or "spirit of poverty" is to understand and accept that just as there are two kingdoms at work in the struggle for our souls (the Kingdom of Darkness and the Kingdom of Light), the same two kingdoms are likewise at work in the area of our finances. These opposing kingdoms include the earthly kingdom of Mammon (or the pull of the culture—characterized by need, lack, deprivation, hunger, insufficiency, fear and poverty) in contrast to God's heavenly economy of Abundance—the mind and heart of God (characterized by abundance, plenty, peace, sufficiency and trust).

Mammon Economy Mammon (or the world's) economy is based upon credit, debt, want, prestige, desire for prosperity, financial stress, worry, fear, greed and covetousness, which are forms of idolatry. God hates idolatry in any and all of its forms. Idolatry is the act of putting someone or something in a higher place of value and respect than where we place God. Note that the first three commandments

> * Unless otherwise noted, Biblical references are taken from the King James Version.

(see Ex. 20) are direct cautions against idolatry. Eph. 5:5 explicitly informs us, "For this ye know, that no whoremonger, nor unclean person, nor covetous man, who is an idolater, hath any inheritance in the kingdom of Christ and of God." Money is the chief rival god, as the use of money for greed, covetousness and/or hoarding is contrary to God's design of sharing, giving and generosity. Greed refers to the desire for extravagant (unnecessary and selfish) wealth and covetousness (in this Biblical context) refers to having an excessive and unregulated (undisciplined) envy with regard to things that do not belong to us. God takes greed and covetousness very seriously.

Mamona is an Aramaic term for wealth. The NIV of the Bible capitalizes "Money" or Mammon because it is a proper name. Mammon is a spiritual person in the demonic world. Mammon produces the "spirit of poverty." Covetousness and greed are characteristics in allegiance to the false god named Mammon. In Scripture, when Jesus mentioned Mammon, it was in the context of not being able to serve two masters.

Serving any supernatural master (like Mammon) in the demonic world is considered hard-core idolatry. Satan wants us to be in bondage to and to serve the "spirit of poverty." Recall the rich young ruler (in Mat. 19:16-22) who came to Jesus and asked what he needed to do in order to inherit eternal life. When Jesus answered him, telling him to sell all that he had and to give to the poor…, Scripture says, "he went away sorrowful: for he had great possessions." This passage points out the rich young ruler's lack— his attachment to wealth (Mammon) being greater than his attachment to God. Consider also the following attributes of poverty.

- Poverty is a tormentor.

- Poverty creates a climate of hopelessness where seeds of suicide grow.

- Poverty strips a man or a woman of their self-confidence and sense of worth.

- Poverty blurs and diminishes visions and dreams.

- Poverty is where the seeds of anger and cynicism grow.

- Poverty is slavery (and financial captivity is unnatural).

- The "spirit of poverty" will make you critical of those who are trying to set you free.

- Poverty will make you question the truth about God, who is your true Source and Provider.

- Poverty births fear, and fear makes you want to hoard—which cuts off supply.

- Poverty is not merely a financial circumstance of your life, it is a spiritual condition of your heart and soul.

- Poverty is a spirit to be cast out. "The Lord is …

	my deliverer …"—Ps. 18:2.

- Poverty is an enemy to be destroyed. Poverty is a curse (see Deut. 28:15, and chapter 30) and was a result of Adam's sin. However, Christ's death on the cross met the demands of justice for the cancellation of the curse of poverty (as exemplified in the Scriptural passage which notes "mercy triumphs over justice"). God's Heavenly Economy of Abundance Unfamiliar to most, God's economy has unlimited resources. Within God's economy, there is no want or lack. God's economy is characterized by sufficiency, plenty, abundance and feelings of peace, contentment and trust. Lovingly, God's economy makes the problems of the economy of Mammon disappear. Recognize that God does His part when we do our part. Consider the following characteristics of God's heavenly economy:

1. God has infinite resources—and as His heirs, all these resources are available to us. For example:

• Ex. 16—in the wilderness, the Israelites were fed manna for 40 years

• 1 Ki. 17:8-16—Elijah and the widow; her oil and meal did not waste, "until" …

• 2 Ki. 4:1-7—Elisha's counsel to the widow; one pot of oil filled many—the oil was sold and the widow's debt was paid

• 1 Chr. 29:3-28—David, although born a poor peasant, gave untold wealth to build the temple, recognizing and acknowledging "all things come of thee" (vs. 14)

• Mat. 14:15-21—Jesus fed 5000 men with 5 loaves and 2 fishes
• Mat. 15:32-38—Jesus fed 4000 men with 7 loaves and "a few little fishes," with 7 full baskets left over

• Mat. 17:24-27—Peter and the coin in the fish

• Luke 5:1-11—Simon Peter casts his net on the other side, and the net almost broke for the abundance of the weight of fish he caught 2. God multiplies rather than adds—In the Mammon economy, 5-10% interest is considered good. Compare this interest with the manifold returns God promises us:

• Gen. 26:12—Isaac was blessed 100-fold

• Gen. 30:27-30—Laban acknowledges the increase of his cattle was because of Jacob's favor with the Lord

• Mat. 13:12 and Mark 4:8—an increase of 30, 60, or 100-fold; "For whosoever hath, to him shall be given, and he shall have more abundance.…"

• Other Scriptures which promise manifold increases: Mat. 19:29 and Mark 10:28-30. Our part in sharing in God's heavenly economy is, FIRST, to make a choice, a commitment and a promise to follow God's plan rather than man's plan—that is, to pursue financial freedom and blessings rather than financial foolishness, as in the admonition in Deut. 11:26, "Behold, I set before you this day a blessing and a curse...." Also, "... I have set before you life and death, blessing and cursing: therefore, choose life, that both thou and thy seed may live"—Deut. 30:19 and vs. 15 (also Jos. 24:15). And, as Mat. 6:24 warns, "No man can serve two masters: for either he will hate the one, and love the other; or else he will hold to the one, and despise the other"—we must choose. We cannot simultaneously operate in the Mammon economy and in God's abundant economy.

2, we must meet the conditions He has stated in His Scriptures for receiving the blessings He has promised. I. What the Scriptures Say about Money

1. The Scriptures say more about money, possessions and stewardship than about any other subject. Consider the following:

2. • 16 of the 38 parables Jesus told were about money or possessions.

3. • Jesus spoke more about money than He did about heaven and hell (combined).

4. • 10% of the Gospels, a full 288 verses, deal with money and possessions.

5. • Within the Scriptural passages of the Bible, there are —500 verses on prayer —less than 500 verses on faith —over 2300 verses on money, possessions and stewardship There are at least four notable explanations why money and material possessions were a constant theme in Jesus' teachings.

6.   a) How we handle our money impacts our relationship and fellowship with God. In Jesus' parable in Luke 16:11, He admonishes, "If therefore ye have not been faithful in the unrighteous mammon, who will commit to your trust the true riches?" This passage speaks to the truth that we will never be able to serve God to our fullest potential until we are faithful in dealing with Mammon.

7.   b) Possessions compete with the Lord—and His will and work—for mastery of our lives. Yet God desires His will to be the first priority of our lives. He wants no other idols to occupy any of our time or attention or acts of worship.

c) Much of life revolves around the use of money. Fortunately, God has adequately prepared us for this undertaking by giving us the Scriptures as our guideline for living.

d) Money and material possessions are the last area of our lives we surrender to God (as in the parable of the rich young ruler—Mat. 19:16-22, and as in our final departure from this life).

Promise Prosperity

Paul, an apostle of Christ Jesus by the will of God, in keeping with the promise of life that is in Christ Jesus, 2 Timothy 1:1

Paul, an apostle of Christ Jesus by the will of God, and Timothy our brother, To the church of God in Corinth, together with all the saints throughout Achaia: 2 Corinthians 1:1

You are all sons of God through faith in Christ Jesus. Galatians 3:26

There is neither Jew nor Greek, slave nor free, male nor female, for you are all one in Christ Jesus. Galatians 3:28

treasuring up for themselves a firm foundation for the future, so that they may take hold of that which is truly life. 1 Timothy 6:19

He has saved us and called us with a holy calling, not because of our own works, but by His own purpose and by the grace He granted us in Christ Jesus before time eternal. 2 Timothy 1:9

And now He has revealed this grace through the appearing of our Savior, Christ Jesus, who has abolished death and illuminated the way to life and immortality through the gospel, 2 Timothy 1:10

God Promise Prosperity to the Obedient. While blessings and curses are direct opposites, they have several things in common. They are words pronounced, decreed or written in the Bible with spiritual power and authority for good (blessings) or for evil (curses). Blessings are mentioned 221 times in the Bible;

curses are mentioned 230 times. Some examples of promised blessings of abundance follow: Blessings mentioned within Deut. 28:1-14 (and curses follow in vs. 15-68)

- We will be "set on high above all nations of the earth."

- We will experience blessings "in the city" and "in the field;" "when we come in" and "when we go out."

- Blessed shall be the fruit of our body.

- Blessed shall be the fruit (produce) of our ground.

- Blessed shall be the offspring (increase) of our cattle and herds.

- Blessed shall be our "basket" (a large container used to store items—i.e., fruit or agricultural products) and "store" (a kneading trough, used at home for storage and for the preparation of foods, particularly bread).

- Blessed shall be our storehouses.

- Blessed shall be anything we set our hand to do.

- Our enemies will be smitten before our faces and shall flee before us.

- The Lord shall make us plenteous in goods.

- The Lord shall open to us His good treasure (rain in due season, etc.).

- We shall lend to many nations, and not borrow; the Lord shall make us the head and not the tail; we shall be above and not beneath these nations Blessings mentioned within Deut. 8:5-18—We are promised:

- To eat bread without scarceness and lack nothing

- The building of goodly houses

- The multiplying of herds and flocks

- The multiplying of silver and gold

- The multiplying of all that we have Blessings mentioned within Mal. 3:8-12 (if we bring the "tithes into the storehouse")

- God will open to us the windows of heaven

- God will pour us out a blessing, that there shall not be room enough to receive it

- God will rebuke the devourer for our sakes

- The devourer shall not destroy the fruits of our ground

- Our vine shall not cast her fruit before the time in the field

- All nations shall call us blessed Other Scriptures Promising Abundance

- Jos. 1:8 "… thou shalt … for then thou shalt make thy way prosperous, and then thou shall have good success."

- Ps. 34:10 "… they that seek the Lord shall not want any good thing."

- Ps. 84:11 "… no good thing will he withhold from them that walk uprightly."

- Is. 1:19 "If ye be willing and obedient, ye shall eat the good of the land…."

- 2 Cor. 8:9 "For ye know the grace of our Lord Jesus Christ, that, though he was rich, yet for your sakes he became poor, that ye through his poverty might be rich."

- Phi. 4:19 "But my God shall supply all your need according to his riches in glory by Christ Jesus."

- 3 John 2 "Beloved, I wish above all things that thou mayest prosper and be in health, even as thy soul prospereth." From the above scriptural passages it should be obvious that God's plan and intention for his people is abundance. There is nothing sacred or desirous about being poor. Being poor is a curse that must be broken; poverty is a "spirit" to be delivered from. Poverty is overcome by generosity. I am sure there are those in Africa who have questioned whether or not the African Bible reads the same as Western Bibles in this regard. Individuals in the West seem to be able to more readily realize the promises of abundance than those in Africa, but I assure you that both Bibles read the same. God made the same promises to Africans that He made to Westerners. God does not lie. The good news is that God has a plan to release you from the "spirit of poverty" and into the realm of abundance. He has a divine plan for managing your finances.

The principles of this plan are contained in the Scriptures. This study is intended to help you better understand and practice, or apply, the principles of that plan. To gain the most from your effort, commit now to read every Scripture listed. While the promised results may not occur overnight, the ultimate blessings are assured. Let's begin with the foundational teachings for how God wants us to think about and use money.

Managing Your Finances

A faithful, sensible servant is one to whom the master can give the responsibility of managing his other household servants and feeding them Matthew 24:45

A king delights in a wise servant, but his anger falls on the shameful. Proverbs 14:35

A faithful man will abound with blessings, but one eager to be rich will not go unpunished. Proverbs 28:20

Therefore everyone who hears these words of Mine and acts on them is like a wise man who built his house on the rock. Matthew 7:24

Look, I am sending you out like sheep among wolves; therefore be as shrewd as snakes and as innocent as doves. Matthew 10:16

Blessed is that servant whose master returns and finds him doing his job. Matthew 24:46

Five of them were foolish, and five were wise. Matthew 25:2

His master replied, 'Well done, good and faithful servant! You have been faithful with a few things; I will put you in charge of many things. Enter into the joy of your master!' Matthew 25:21

Foundational Teachings of Managing Your Finances There are seven foundational principles on which God's plan for our finances is based. These divine principles are Scriptural concepts which need to be understood, accepted and applied, in order for the promised blessings to occur.

1. God Created Everything—In the beginning there was nothing; God created everything (Gen. 1). You and I were born with "nothing" and will leave this world with "nothing." We need to recognize and appreciate that God gave us everything we have. All we possess is His, not ours; instead, we are users, managers and stewards, but not owners.

2. God Owns Everything—Everything that is created is owned by God. While we may consider our possessions as being exclusively "ours," this belief is a misconception shared by our current culture, and it is the root of the problem we face in our attempt to manage money God's way. As identified in Scripture, God owns:
- The earth Ps. 24:1
- All the gold and silver Hag. 2:8
- All that is in heaven and earth 1 Chr. 29:11
- The land Lev. 25:23
- The cattle on a thousand hills Ps. 50:10
- Other scriptures affirming God's ownership include: Ex. 9:29 Deut. 8:18 Deut. 10:14 1 Chr. 29:12 Ps. 24:1 1 Cor. 10:26

3. We Are Stewards/Managers/Trustees—Flowing out of the fact that God created and owns everything is the logical conclusion that whatsoever

we possess is not really ours but is God's; we are simply entrusted with earthly possessions. We are not owners; we are stewards/managers/trustees. Trustees have no rights; instead, trustees have responsibilities.

To be successful in implementing God's plan, we need to develop a steward's mindset. Review the following insights, which verify our role as steward/manager/trustee and to God's role as owner:
• The Parable of the Tenants (or Vineyard; Mat. 21:33-46 and Mark 12:1-12)
• Culturally and historically, the Israelites respected God as owner; the concept of individual ownership came out of Rome.
• 1 Cor. 4:2, "Moreover, it is required in stewards that a man be found faithful."

4. God Gives To Each According To His Plan—Besides being creator and owner, God is ultimately in control of every event that occurs upon the earth. He is God of the universe, of nations and of each of us as individuals. According to Scripture, He "establishes" nations and kings and "removes" them at His will. In addition, He gives us resources according to His individual plan for us. Scriptural passages to review include:
• Is. 40:15-26—God controls nations
• Mat. 25:14-30—the Parable of the Talents
• 1 Chr. 29:12—"riches and honor come of thee, and thou reignest over all"
• Deut. 8:18—it is God that giveth the power to get wealth…
• Dan. 2:21,44—God sets up and deposes kings
We must learn to be content with God's provision (as Paul confessed—"Not that I speak in respect of

want; for I have learned, in whatsoever state I am, therewith to be content"—Phi. 4:11), to be content with our present level of abundance. Contentment is mentioned seven times in the entire Bible, and in six of those seven times it relates to money. Additionally, within the curses noted in Deut. 28:47-48,

we discover the importance of having an attitude of being a "cheerful receiver": "Because thou servedst not the Lord thy God with joyfulness, and with gladness of heart, for the abundance of all things, Therefore shalt thou serve thine enemies which the Lord shall send against thee, in hunger, and in thirst, and in nakedness, and in want of all things: and he shall put a yoke of iron upon thy neck, until he have destroyed thee."

5. Scripture Mentions Three Levels of provision—Notwithstanding God gives to each according to His plan, there are three "levels of provision" mentioned in the Bible. His plan is for us to be in sufficiency or abundance. Where do you presently find yourself?

- In Poverty—in need, naked, hungry, thirsty
- In Sufficiency—have enough, but none to spare
- In Abundance/Prosperity—enough and to spare (notice, this is not the same as being "wealthy") We have mentioned previously that Jesus atoned for the "curse of poverty" on the cross. God's promise of abundance will not move you from poverty to prosperity in a moment of time. It takes time and effort to store His words in our heart.

Even so—as promised in Jer. 31:33— He writes His words (law) on our heart: "… I will put my law in their inward parts, and write it in their hearts; and will be their God, and they shall be my people." Or, as also stated in Heb. 10:16, "... I will put my laws into their hearts, and in their minds will I write them...." (See also Jos. 1:8, "This book of the law shall not depart out of thy mouth; but thou shalt meditate therein day and night, that thou mayest observe to do according to all that is written therein: for then thou shalt make thy way prosperous, and then thou shalt have good success.") It takes time and effort to become a good manager over what God has provided.

Remember, too, that God is not a heavenly ATM machine from which you can withdraw cash whenever you need it, as He oftentimes will "prove" you—or first give you a little amount to see how you manage your allotment of money. 6. God Wants You to Have "Finances" in Order to (while the primary reason God wants you to have abundance is because He loves His children, there are other reasons, as identified below)—

• Provide for the needs of your own family and household (1 Tim. 5:8)

• Complete your current and progressing assignments

• Assist in sending ministers, evangelists, etc., throughout the world to preach the gospel (Rom. 10:15) • Pay your taxes to your government and your obligations to God (Mat. 22:21)

• Return tithe back to God's house—for the work of the Lord (Lev. 27:30)

• Give good gifts to your children and to those you love (Mat. 7:11)

• Give to others who need to complete their assignments

• Increase your giving to help the poor (Pro. 11:24-26, 19:17 and 28:27)

• Solve any emergency or crisis that arises (Eccl. 10:19b)

• Dream dreams big enough for you, your family and others—dreams which require the supernatural intervention of God 7. God Blesses the Obedient— One of the fundamental principles about "blessings" most overlooked in the Bible is that of conditional promises. Bible scholars list some 635 promised blessings for us as individuals. Without exception, ALL of them are conditional. That is, the Lord promises us that He will do something (blessing) if we will do something first (obedience). Take, for example, the promise of salvation. While Jesus died on the cross for all, the promise of salvation is conditional upon us: "That if thou shalt confess with thy mouth the Lord Jesus, and shalt believe in thine heart that God hath raised him from the dead, thou shalt be saved"—Rom. 10:9. Thus "all" are not "recipients" of Jesus' sacrifice on the cross, until they first do their part as provided in Rom. 10:9 above.

Take another example—that of being "born again." Note the specified "condition" which comes before the promise: "Except a man be born of water and of the Spirit, he cannot enter into the kingdom of God"—John 3:5. Thus, all are not born again until they are born of water and of the Spirit. The same holds true of the promises and blessings given for a life of abundance. We cannot expect to receive the promises until we meet the conditions God has put forth in His Word. If we are disobedient, we have no promise and in many cases bring upon ourselves, instead, a curse.

The Bible lists 37 groups of "sins of disobedience" that result in cursing. Consistently, according to God's plan, these curses are not removed without repentance and obedience. "But it shall come to pass, if thou wilt not hearken unto the voice of the LORD thy God, to observe to do all his commandments and his statutes which I command thee this day; that all these curses shall come upon thee, and overtake thee"—Deut. 28:15 (see also Deut. 8:10-20; 27:15- 26 and 28:15-68). Because the blessings mentioned in Scripture are conditional, they are only attainable by those who are obedient. There are no such promises for those who are disobedient; in fact, curses are what are promised. If you want what God has – you must do what God says.

Conditions Required for Receiving the Blessings and Promises of Abundance Let's consider several conditions noted in Scripture for receiving the blessings and promises of abundance:

1. Paying Your Tithes and Making Offerings— Paying tithing is not an option; Deut. 14:22 commands us to tithe. We must understand, acknowledge and live by the fact that, besides being "holy," the tithe is the Lord's (Lev. 27:30). In essence, it is our heavenly "rent" for the space we occupy and the possessions the Lord allows us to use. It is a debt and it belongs to God. If you tithe, God will bless you and will "open the windows of heaven" for you. If you don't tithe, your finances will be cursed and the devourer will destroy your fruits. It's that simple. Mal. 3:10 is the only verse in Scripture which tells us to "prove" (test) God. Consider the following about the tithe:

- "Giving" of tithes and offerings is the only real evidence of love (as witnessed in John 3:16)
- The act of paying tithe is evidence we have conquered greed.
- If we do not pay our tithe, we are robbing God of what is rightfully His (Mal. 3). The payment of tithe and "heave offerings" was recognition of Israel's subjection to God—that He owned them and all they had. To withhold the tithe is to renounce the sovereign authority of God, which is to be guilty of the same sin as Lucifer's (in the beginning).
- The act of paying tithe breaks the financial curse which is over our life and our family (Mal. 3).

- The act of paying tithe is acknowledgment of our belief and trust in God. Let's review what the Old Testament reveals concerning tithe: Tithing in the Old Testament (OT) While we generally consider the "tithe" to be 10%, there were at least three tithes commanded by God and several "festival" celebrations (which normally lasted 7 days) wherein additional offerings were required, as noted below:

- A First Tithe (Gen. 14:17-24)—Abraham first gave tithes to Melchizedek; he did not take the spoils. Several Scriptures identify that the Israelites were commanded to tithe a tenth of all their increase (Lev. 27:30 and 32; Deut. 14:22)

- A Levite Tithe (Num. 18:21-24)—also considered a "heave offering" (vs. 24), the Levite tithe was given to support the Levites, who in turn gave a tenth to the priests
- A Welfare Tithe (Deut. 26:12-13)—was required every three year's; it was a "poor man's tithe"
- The Feast of Unleavened Bread (Ex. 12:17)—in remembrance of the Passover
- A Feast of Weeks (Harvest) (Ex. 23:16 and Deut. 16:10)—a first-fruits offering given in remembrance of—and honoring—God, who gave the harvest

- Feast of Trumpets of New Moon (Ps. 81:3)—a reminder of the mighty voice of God
- Feast of the Day of Atonement (Lev. 23:27-28 and Num. 29:12)—a celebration of the covering for sins
- Feast of Tabernacles (Lev. 23:34 and Deut. 16:13-14)—celebrated at the end of the year when all of the labors of the field had been gathered in Biblical scholars have calculated that these individual tithes and offerings account for a total yearly amount of 23.3%. Within this group of tithes and offerings, we see that these required gifts were much more like a "tax," in that this directive was not "voluntary." Let's now review the conditions noted in Mal. 3:8-11: "Will a man rob God? Yet ye have robbed me. But ye say, Wherein have we robbed thee? In tithes and offerings.

(9) Ye are cursed with a curse: for ye have robbed me, even this whole nation.

(10) Bring ye all the tithes into the storehouse, that there may be meat in mine house, and prove me now herewith, saith the Lord of hosts, if I will not open you the windows of heaven, and pour you out a blessing, that there shall not be room enough to receive it.

(11) And I will rebuke the devourer for your sakes, and he shall not destroy the fruits of your ground; neither shall your vine cast her fruit before the time in the field, saith the Lord of hosts." Although God is herein speaking to the nation of Israel, we know that all Scripture is given for the profit of mankind (noted in 2 Tim. 3:16, "All scripture is given by inspiration of God, and is profitable for doctrine, for reproof, for correction, for instruction in righteousness"). Therefore, in this Scriptural passage (Mal. 3:8-11), God is also speaking to us, communicating principles which are

to be guides for a keeper or custodian (a manager or a trustee).

Briefly, God is expressing the pronouncement that if you have not paid your tithing nor consistently made offerings, you have robbed God, and are under a curse (namely, He will leave the devourer at your door). This curse is a disobedience curse, and no amount of prayer by anyone will release you from this curse (for more on Disobedience Curses, refer to this chapter in Healing of the Spirit). The only course of release from this curse is obedience (i.e. "paying" your tithes and "making" your offerings consistently). After God proclaims we have robbed Him, He tells us in vs. 10 how to rectify our sin: "Bring ye all the tithes into the storehouse…" (Note that Mal. 3:9 is the only place in the Bible where God says "prove" [test] me.) Yet look at the numerous blessings promised to those who are obedient in Mal. 3:10-11: " . . . open you the windows of heaven, and pour you out a blessing, that there shall not be room enough to receive it. (11) …

I will rebuke the devourer for your sakes, and he shall not destroy the fruits of your ground; neither shall your vine cast her fruit before the time." What a promise! Unfortunately, most Christians (including many pastors around the world) either don't pay tithing at all or pay it infrequently.

It should be no surprise, then, that those who do not pay their tithe are suffering from poverty. And they will continue to suffer in this way until they begin to faithfully pay and return to God that which is rightfully His. If you want to observe the blessings that can result from paying tithe, refer to the incident recorded in 2 Chr. 31:7-12. In my experience, I have never found a person who, after beginning to tithe and experiencing the blessings and benefits of it, ever quit.

God will bless you far beyond your tithe; and every time you increase your tithe, He blesses you more in return. Let it be sufficiently said that tithing is what belongs to God for the space you occupy on the earth—"rent" for the use of what He has given you. Although the giving of offerings is optional; the giving of tithing is not.

It's all His. God wants increase (Remember the Parable of the Talents?); He wants to be paid. If He is, you are blessed. If He isn't, you are cursed. It's as simple as that. He is very jealous of what is His. When you input the tithing due to God into the Mammon economy, God gets upset, just as you would be upset if you were owed funds from someone who refused to pay you, but who instead spent it on other things.

2. Give a "firstfruits" offering ("first-fruits:" the first grain or fruit harvested each year—considered sacred and offered to God in thanksgiving and celebration in a special ceremony held on the Day of First-fruits) Pro. 3:9-10 encourages us to, "Honour the LORD with thy substance, and with the first-fruits of all thine increase: So shall thy barns be filled with plenty, and thy presses shall burst out with new wine." God requires that we give our tithes and offerings first before we pay anything else; this is why it is referred to as "first-fruits." If we wait until the end of the month to contribute, there is

seldom enough money (or goods) left; then we are giving our "leftovers." If we pay our tithes and offerings at the time we receive an income, honoring God first, there will always be enough to pay for our necessities.

Scriptures Requiring our First-fruits Scriptures Identifying Promised Blessings of Obedience Ex. 22:29 and 23:19 2 Chr. 31:5-8 (so leaders can be encouraged) Lev. 23:10-11 Neh. 13:31 (so the Lord will remember you) Num. 18:12 Pro. 3:9-10 (so thy barns be filled with plenty) Deut. 18:4 and 26:2 Ez. 20:40-41 and 44:30 (for "the blessing of Neh. 10:35-37 and 12:44 peace to rest in thine house")

3. Give to the poor—Consider the following Scriptures which command us to provide for the poor. The poor and widows hold a special place with God. He blesses those that provide for them.

• Deut. 15:7-11 Commandment to give to thy poor and needy brethren.

• Ps. 41:1-3 A blessing for considering the poor.

• Prov. 19:17 "He that hath pity upon the poor lendeth unto the Lord; and that which he hath given will he pay him again."

• Prov. 21:13 "Whoso stoppeth his ears at the cry of the poor, he also shall cry himself, but shall not be heard."

• Prov 22:22-23 "Rob not the poor, because he is poor: neither oppress the afflicted in the gate...."

• Prov. 28:27 "He that giveth unto the poor shall not lack: but he that hideth his eyes shall have many a curse."

• Prov. 29:7 "The righteous considereth the cause of the poor: but the wicked regardeth not to know it."

• Ez. 16:49 One of the causes of Sodom's destruction was not giving to the poor. 4. GIVE—We will reap what we sow—In addition to providing for the poor, for widows and orphans, God gives us the opportunity to give ... and to reap bountifully if we do. • Luke 6:38—"Give, and it shall be given unto you; ... running over...."

• Pro. 11:25—"The liberal soul shall be made fat...."

• 2 Cor. 9:6—"... He which soweth sparingly shall reap also sparingly; and he which soweth bountifully shall reap also bountifully."

• 2 Cor. 9:10—He shall "multiply your seed sown." God's principle of abundance is based upon the concept of sowing in faith and reaping financial blessings. There is another principle teaching called "seed faith." Space, does not allow a full discussion here, but the following are principles of that teaching.

• God commanded everything He created to multiply and become more (Gen. 1:11, 20 and 22).

• Something within you requires increase.

• Every seed contains a seemingly invisible instruction to reproduce more of its own kind.

• When you let go (plant) of the seed in your hand, God will let go of what is in His hand.

• A little seed can birth a huge harvest.

• When you keep what is in your hand, God will keep what is in His hand.

• When you increase the size of your seed-planting, you increase the size of your harvest (2 Cor. 9:6).

• A seed never planted guarantees a season of no harvest.

• Everything you have is a seed; if you keep it, that is your harvest.

- No one else can sow your seed for you.
- When you give your seed a specific assignment, incredible faith is unleashed (1 Ki. 17:13-16).
- Recognize the seed (gift, skill, talent, time, love, money) you have already received from God and thank Him for it (obeying the Law of Thankfulness).
- Thankfulness is a force, a law of the universe; without gratitude you do not harvest.
- Time is currency on earth and can produce what money cannot buy.
- There is a time for planting seeds; if the planting time is missed, so is the harvest.
- Sow what you have been given, and don't complain that you don't have more.
- When you sow, wrap your faith around your seed. Your seed is what God multiplies: but your faith is why He multiplies it.
- God does not recognize need; He only recognizes faith.
- "Seed-faith" is the process of sowing what you have been given, in order to create something else that you have been promised.
- " …with the same measure that ye mete withal it shall be measured to you again"— Luke 6:38.
- Asking is the key to receiving (Mat. 7:7-8 and Jam. 4:2-3).
- Faith requires an instruction—something specific (an amount or a result).
- When you make a seed faith promise, you've entered into a covenant between you and God. Don't ever be a promise-breaker with God.
- Crisis is the place of miracles, but "fear" gets in the way. (FEAR: false evidence appearing real)

- Waiting is the forgotten (but powerful) season between sowing and reaping.
- Some of the greatest blessings come after the longest waiting.
- If you dig up your seed to re-examine it because of impatience, there may not be any harvest.
- The size of your seed determines the size of your harvest.
- Save the tithe from Satan; either it is given to God or it will be collected by Satan.
- Until a Christian has experienced freedom in the area of money, he will never experience God's total plan for his life.
- Your tongue determines your harvest. You reap what you speak (Jam. 3:3-6).

For more on "seed faith," the Reasons People Do Not Receive Their Financial Harvest. As a steward, be a good manager and/or trustee of God's possessions—("Moreover it is required in stewards, that a man be found faithful"—1 Cor. 4:2.) Possession is not necessarily ownership. If we believe God owns it all, then we must accept our role and part as managers and stewards. Review the parable of the vineyard (Mark 12:1-9 and Luke 20:9-16). When we acknowledge God's ownership, every spending decision becomes a spiritual decision. Good stewards will:

a) Live by the 10-10-80 rule. From their income, good stewards will pay 10% tithing as their first-fruits, they'll save 10% and they'll live on the remaining 80%.
b) b) Keep good records of their income and expenses.
c) c) Not borrow and make every effort to live debt-free. The Mammon economy is based

upon credit and debt. While Scripture does not call debt a sin, "surety"—or the taking on of an obligation to pay, without a certain way to repay—is seriously discouraged (refer to Prov. 11:15, 17:18 and 22:26-27). Borrowing is authorized only for items that appreciate and are always worth more than what you owe on them, such as houses. We are, however, in financial bondage when we are in debt and are not entirely free to do what the Lord wants us to do because of our indebtedness. Debt may delay God's plan for your life; it can also disrupt spiritual growth. Review the following passages:

d) • Deut. 15:6 and 28:12 "… thou shalt not borrow…."

• Prov. 22:7 "The rich ruleth over the poor, and the borrower is servant to the lender." • Rom. 13:8 "Owe no man anything…." d) Limit spending to needs and "just" wants. The Mammon economy is driven by satisfying our wants and desires (not only "just" or fair wants but all things "unjust" and extravagant as well). Functioning within God's economy is accomplished by making careful choices and decisions about the difference between our needs and our "just" wants and desires (as in 1 Tim. 6:8). Our focus should be to discipline ourselves to manage our surplus in a manner designed of God.

e) Ask God before you spend or invest in a business. If you do not have the funds to do what you want to do, perhaps the Lord is telling you to wait. If you feel the Lord is speaking to you about investing in a business, seek sound counsel during your pursuit of this endeavor. Ask for the advice of at least two witnesses or individuals before you proceed. Make sure it is God who is telling you to continue—not something from your own spirit.

6. **Faithfulness in Little**—Luke 16:10-12 counsels us: "He that is faithful in that which is least is faithful also in much: and he that is unjust in the least is unjust also in much. If therefore ye have not been faithful in the unrighteous mammon, who will commit to your trust the true riches? And if ye have not been faithful in that which is another man's, who shall give you that which is your own?" One of the reasons you may not have abundance is because God cannot yet trust you with heavenly abundance. Before God will allow you to be His manager over the riches of heaven, you will need to show God you are a good manager/steward/trustee of the unrighteous mammon within your possession, as indicated in the following passage: "And the Lord said, Who then is that faithful and wise steward, whom his lord shall make ruler over his household, to give them their portion of meat in due season? Blessed is that servant, whom his lord when he cometh shall find so doing.

Of a truth I say unto you, that he will make him ruler over all that he hath. But and if that servant say in his heart, My lord delayeth his coming; and shall begin to beat the menservants and maidens, and to eat and drink, and to be drunken; The lord of that servant will come in a day when he looketh not for him, and at an hour when he is not aware, and will cut him in sunder, and will appoint him his portion with the unbelievers. And that servant, which knew his lord's will, and prepared not himself, neither did according to his will, shall be beaten with many stripes. But he that knew not, and did commit things worthy of stripes, shall be beaten with few stripes. For unto whomsoever much is given, of him shall be much required: and to whom men have committed much, of him they will ask the more"—Luke 12:42-48. Several scriptures require us to be good stewards. We are God's "agents." An agent is one who acts on behalf of the wishes of an owner. The way you spend your money is an indication of your relationship (faithful or foolish) with God.

Curses of Witchcraft

I will destroy your witchcraft and you will no longer cast spells. Micah 5:12

Both of these will overtake you in a moment, on a single day: loss of children and widowhood. They will come upon you in full measure, in spite of your many sorceries and all your potent spells. Isaiah 47:9

idolatry and witchcraft; hatred, discord, jealousy, fits of rage, selfish ambition, dissensions, factions Galatians 5:20

Let no one be found among you who sacrifices his son or daughter in the fire, practices divination or conjury, interprets omens, practices sorcery, Deuteronomy 18:10

Though these nations you shall dispossess listen to conjurers and diviners, the LORD your God has not permitted you to do so. Deuteronomy 18:14

For You have abandoned Your people, the house of Jacob, because they are filled with influences from the east; they are soothsayers like the Philistines; they strike hands with the children of foreigners. Isaiah 2:6

When men tell you to consult the spirits of the dead and the spiritists who whisper and mutter, shouldn't a people consult their God instead? Why consult the dead on behalf of the living? Isaiah 8:19

Curses of Witchcraft, Traditional Medicines and Family Celebrations In many cities, experience has proven that the curse of poverty comes about as the result of believers being directly subjected to the dark spirits of witchcraft, of traditional medicines, of family celebrations (demonic in nature), of polygamy, and of immorality—or believers are the recipient of generational curses such as the cultural "spirit of pauper" that are passed down through the family line (from an ancestor's exposure to these dark spirits).

Steps for obtaining spiritual freedom (as listed in Healing of the Spirit) should be followed— first achieving release from these spirits (noted in the previous paragraph) before deliverance from the curse of poverty is addressed. Even if the believer complies with the promises to receive the "spirit of provision," there may yet be no breakthrough if there are still curses remaining from previous exposure to witchcraft, traditional medicines, family celebrations, polygamy or immorality. Until all these curses are broken, and there is freedom from these dark spirits, the "spirit of provision" is not able to enter. The order of this process is very important. In preparation for a seminar, as I was solemnly praying about the "curse of poverty" over Africa, the Lord revealed to me that the "spirit of poverty" must be prayed against in the same way that other spirits of darkness are prayed against.

Namely, through

(1) confession,

(2) repentance,

(3) removal of any existing spiritual permission previously given to the "spirit of poverty" and giving permission for possession back to Jesus, and finally,

(4) commanding the spirit(s) to leave. Pray the following prayer only after prayers for freedom from witchcraft, traditional

medicines, family celebrations and polygamy have been successfully offered.

Prayer for Release from the Curse of Poverty Lord Jesus, I come before You now to be delivered from the "curse of poverty."

I confess that I've regrettably traded the value of the Kingdom of Heaven for the desires of my heart in the form of earthly treasures. Lord, I repent for worrying about life, food and clothing.

I repent for laying-up treasures on earth where moths and rust destroy and where thieves break in and steal. Lord,

I repent for loving money, for serving Mammon (the dark spirit of riches), for greed and for covetousness—all forms of idolatry.

I repent of the belief that money is the answer to everything lacking in my life.

I repent for forsaking You as my life source and for focusing my eyes on the pursuit of provisions to my own harm and the harm of others.

I repent for choosing to serve Mammon in preference to You and thereby filling my life with darkness, bondage and stress.

I repent for being double-minded with how I value money and unstable in all my ways. I choose to hate Mammon and to love You, Lord, with all my heart.

I choose to place my treasure where my heart is, in the Kingdom of Heaven, for You to use as You choose.

I acknowledge and confess my own sins of poverty for robbing God of tithes and offerings and for not paying the first-fruits of all that You have given me, for not providing for widows, orphans and the poor and for not being faithful even in a little. Lord, forgive me for these sins in order that I might be set free from this curse, in Jesus' name. Ancestors I stand in the stead of my ancestors to confess and repent for their robbing God of tithes and offerings and for not paying their first-fruits of all that You gave them.

I repent for myself and for my generational line for hardening my heart and shutting my hand against my brothers and sisters in their need and for not feeding, nor taking care of, the widows and orphans. Lord, I ask Your forgiveness for my ancestors' sins in order that I might be set free from this curse.

I repent with all my heart across my generational line for pride and vain striving for silver and gold and for seeking earthly treasures. I choose to seek after the ultimate treasure of my Lord Jesus Christ.

I repent for myself and for my family line for making any material possessions or things an idol in my life.

Poverty Mindset Lord, the devil has decreed death and destruction over my life; he desires that my portion be poverty and hopelessness. On my behalf and on that of my ancestors I repent for believing in a poverty mindset, in the culture of the pauper spirit, for coming into agreement with lack, for giving myself to materialism and greed, and for being stingy with the body of Christ.

I repent and confess the lie— that godliness implies living in poverty and lacking basic necessities, that it implies the requirement to live in the state of poverty and always be in need. Father, in Your mercy, free me and my future generations of the consequences of this lie and portion, and may all praise and honor be repeatedly given to You for the abundant blessings I know You have in store for me and for my family

Giving Lord, I repent for making my tithing and my giving "an obligation" to You and for not giving as a free act of my love. Lord, remove the canopy of law and obligation and the yoke of law and obligation from me. Lord, allow me to live in Your grace and under Your provision. As Your Word professes, the generous soul will be made rich, and he who waters will also be watered himself. He who sows bountifully will reap bountifully—in full measure—pressed down and running over. Lord, I revoke any spiritual permission I have given the spirit of poverty and return it to you. Declaration I declare that Jesus came to give us abundant life.

  I choose to believe, accept and trust that God will supply all my needs, that there will be an inheritance for me and for my descendants, that none will be in poverty, and that, instead, all their needs will be met. I choose to be connected to the "river of life," where God grants the ability to acquire wealth for His kingdom.

  I will open my hand and heart to the poor and the needy, generously sharing my resources as You lead me, so no-one will lack, and so Your power will not be hindered and Your grace will remain. Lord, I ask You to destroy the connectors and cleanse the lines attached between me and earthly treasurers. Lord, connect me to You alone.

  I choose not to hold onto anything but You. I give everything I have to You. You are the owner of all I have. Lord, allow me to live within Your grace and provision. Lord, I repent for not trusting You or Your provision for me.

  I will trust in You to provide for all my needs. I declare I will be content in You and in my wages in whatsoever financial state I find myself. Lord, thank You for giving me the creativity to produce abundance through sowing my seed. Holy Spirit, teach me what to sow, what to reap, and what to harvest for divine purposes.

  I declare that I will eat the bread of life and delight in your abundance. Lord, help me to see money in all its aspects with spiritual eyes, knowing it is Your resource, that it belongs to You for whatever purposes You intend. Lord, I ask that You release the resources that the enemy has stolen from me and my family line. Lord, break off the curses of sowing much and bringing in little, of eating and not having enough, and of earning wages only to put them into a bag with holes. May You also restore the harvests that the locusts have eaten. Thank You, Lord.

I repent for myself and my family line for not receiving the rich inheritance You have for us in Your promise: to open the windows of heaven and pour out a blessing that we are unable to receive.

I promise to fulfill my part of the conditions that I might receive these blessings and this inheritance—the abundance and gifts You have for us. I ask that these blessings come in such abundance that we will be able to leave a rich inheritance (of teachings as well as material gifts) to my children and grandchildren. Lord Jesus, I make the following confessions of belief:

- I believe Jesus died on the cross for my poverty.

- I believe His atonement provided for my abundance.

- I believe Jesus took on the curse of poverty for me.

- I believe that though Christ was rich, yet for our sakes He became poor, that through His poverty I might become rich (2 Cor. 8:9).

- I believe that God owns everything on the earth, that I am a manager and steward; all I have belongs to Him.

- I believe God owns all the silver and gold and all the cattle on a thousand hills, that He has infinite resources in heaven.

- I believe Jesus will meet all my needs from His abundance in heaven.

- I believe God's promises for provision are conditional.

- I believe the Bible promises abundance, if I meet the prescribed conditions.

- I believe God shall provide for all my needs according to His riches in glory by Christ Jesus (Phil. 4:19).

- I believe that I must pay tithes and offerings in order to receive the abundance of Heaven.

- I believe that if I am obedient, God will remove the devourer from my door. Promises And now, Oh Lord, I promise before You and these witnesses to:

- Pay tithing and offerings of all I receive

- Pay first-fruits of all I receive

- Give to support my church pastor, widows, orphans and the poor and needy

- Trust You for my provision

- Live on the 10-10-80 plan You have designed

- Wait for You to open the doors for job or business pursuits

- Give You thanks before I receive and give You all the Glory Your Word I declare that your Word says: You will give us the treasures of heaven and hidden riches of secret places. You are the One who gives power to get wealth, that You may establish Your covenant which You swore to our fathers, as it is this day. Jesus,

I release "the spirit of Asher† Father, give me a circumcised heart so You can release Your treasures from heaven. Lord, increase us more and more—me and my children.

I beseech thee, send now prosperity in the name of Jesus. anointing" and "the anointing to be an overcomer"—to have a breakthrough mentality.

Father, I—and the generations which come after me—will not be beneath; we will be above. We will be the head and not the tail.

I am blessed and highly favored of the Lord. I come against the "spirit of poverty" and Mammon, and I command them to go.

I command the "spirit of poverty" to go—to get off my wallet, to get out of my checking account, to get off of and out of my home, to get out of my family, to get out of my business pursuits and to get out of my church.

I solemnly declare that I have no agreement with you! I ask for the "spirit of provision" and the "spirit of giving" to come into my life and under my domain. Lord,

I pray that You will restore what the locusts have eaten and that which has been stolen, taken or lost. Restore me to my rightful place as an heir of the abundance of the Kingdom of God. All praise be to You, Lord, as You release my provision in Jesus' name. AMEN

SPECIFIC POSSESSIONS GOD OWNS

1. The land, moreover, shall not be sold permanently, for the land is Mine (Leviticus 25:23).
2. Gold and silver You also took your beautiful jewels made of My gold and of My silver, which I had given you, and made for yourself male images that you might play the harlot with them (Ezekiel 16:17).
3. "The silver is Mine, and the gold is Mine," declares the Lord of hosts (Haggai 2:8).
4. Animals For every beast of the forest is Mine, the cattle on a thousand hills. I know every bird of the mountains, and everything that moves in the fields is Mine (Psalm 50:10-11).

GOD CONTROLS EVERY EVENT

LORD CONTROLS ALL EVENTS ON EARTH

Yours is the dominion, O Lord, and You exalt Yourself as head over all. Both riches and honor come from You, and You rule over all, and in Your hand is power and might; and it lies in Your hand to make great, and to strengthen everyone (1 Chronicles 29:11-12). Whatever the Lord pleases, He does, in heaven and in earth (Psalm 135:6). The lot is cast into the lap, but its every decision is from the Lord (Proverbs 16:33). Man's steps are ordained by the Lord, how then can man understand his way? (Proverbs 20:24). Daniel answered and said, "Let the name of God be blessed forever... it is He who changes the times and the epochs; He removes kings and establishes kings (Daniel 2:20-21).

Lord allows difficult circumstances to occur Then all his [Job's] brothers, and all his sisters, and all who had known him before, came to him, and they ate bread with him in his house; and they consoled him and comforted him for all the evil that the Lord had brought on him (Job 42:11). I am the Lord, and there is no other, the One forming light and creating darkness, causing wellbeing and creating calamity; I am the Lord who does all these (Isaiah 45:6-7). Who is there who speaks and it comes to pass, unless the Lord has commanded it? Is it not from the mouth of the Most High that both good and ill go forth? (Lamentations 3:37-38). If a calamity occurs in a city has not the Lord done it? (Amos 3:6).

• Lord uses every circumstances for a good purpose in the life of the godly We know that God causes all things to work together for good to those who love God, to those who are called according to His purpose (Romans 8:28).

• Example of Lord allowing difficult circumstances for ultimate good Do not be grieved or angry with yourselves, because you sold me here; for God sent me before you to preserve life. For the famine has been in the land these two years, and there are still five years in which there will be neither plowing nor harvesting. And God sent me before you to preserve for you a remnant in the earth, and to keep you alive by a great deliverance.

Now, therefore, it was not you who sent me here, but God; and He has made me a father to Pharaoh and lord of all his household and ruler over all the land of Egypt. Hurry and go up to my father, and say to him, 'Thus says your son Joseph, "God has made me lord of all Egypt (Genesis 45:5-9).

A carnal person's perspective of the control of events I again saw under the sun that the race is not to the swift, and the battle is not to the warriors, and neither is bread to the wise, nor wealth to the discerning, nor favor to men of ability; for time and chance overtake them all (Ecclesiastes 9:11).

SPECIFIC EVENTS AND ITEMS LORD CONTROLS

1. Lord directs people's hearts The king's heart is like channels of water in the hand of the Lord; He turns it wherever He wishes (Proverbs 21:1).

• Lord can give godly people favor with others The Lord was with Joseph and extended kindness to him, and gave him favor in the sight of the chief jailer (Genesis 39:21). The Lord had caused them to rejoice, and had turned the heart of the king of Assyria toward them to encourage them in the work of the house of God, the God of Israel (Ezra 6:22). The king granted them [Nehemiah's requests] to me because the good hand of my God was on me... I told them how the hand of my God had been favorable to me (Nehemiah 2:8, 18).

• Example of Israelites plundering Egyptians I [the Lord] will grant this people favor in the sight of the Egyptians; and it shall be that when you go, you will not go empty-handed. But every woman shall ask of her neighbor and the woman who lives in her house, articles of silver and articles of gold, and clothing; and you will put them on your sons and daughters. Thus you will plunder the Egyptians (Exodus 3:21-22). Now the sons of Israel had done according to the word of Moses, for they had requested from the Egyptians articles of silver and articles of gold, and clothing; and the Lord had given the people favor in the sight of the Egyptians, so that they let them have their request. Thus they plundered the Egyptians (Exodus 12:35-36).

• Lord makes some people obstinate Thus I will harden Pharaoh's heart, and he will chase after them; and I will be honored through Pharaoh and all his army, and the Egyptians will know that I am the Lord (Exodus 14:4). Sihon king of Heshbon was not willing for us to pass through his land; for the Lord your God hardened his spirit and made his heart obstinate, in order to deliver him into your hand, as he is today (Deuteronomy 2:30).

• Lord controls the coveting of the heart Three times a year all your males are to appear before the Lord God, the God of Israel. For I will drive out nations before you and enlarge your borders, and no man shall covet your land when you go up three times a year to appear before the Lord your God (Exodus 34:23-24).

Lord controls the nations

He made from one, every nation of mankind to live on all the face of the earth, having determined their appointed times, and the boundaries of their habitation (Acts 17:26). "O king, do not let the army of Israel go with you, for the Lord is not with Israel nor with any of the sons of Ephraim... God will bring you down before the enemy, for God has power to help and to bring down" (2 Chronicles 25:7-9). Woe to Assyria, the rod of My anger... I sent it against a godless nation and commission it against the people of My fury to capture booty and to seize plunder (Isaiah 10:5-6).

AMOUNT TO GIVE A TITHE

1. Before the law [Abram] gave him [Melchizedek] a tenth of all (Genesis 14:20). Then Jacob made a vow, saying, "If God will be with me and will keep me on this journey... all that You give me I will surely give a tenth to You" (Genesis 28:20-22).

2. Under the law Thus all the tithe of the land, of the seed of the land or of the fruit of the tree, is the Lord's; it is holy to the Lord... every tenth part of herd or flock, whatever passes under the rod, the tenth one shall be holy to the Lord (Leviticus 27:30-32).

• Not tithing considered robbing God Will a man rob God? Yet you are robbing Me! But you say, 'How have we robbed You?" In tithes and offerings. You are cursed with a curse, for you are robbing Me, the whole nation of you! (Malachi 3:8-9).

• Tithe eaten in presence of Lord You shall surely tithe all the produce from what you sow, which comes out of the field every year. And you shall eat in the presence of the Lord your God, at the place where He chooses to establish His name, the tithe of your grain, your new wine, your oil, and the first-born of your herd and your flock, in order that you may learn to fear the Lord your God always. And if the distance is so great for you that you are not able to bring the tithe, since the place where the Lord your God chooses to set His name is too far away from you when the Lord your God blesses you, then you shall exchange it for money, and bind the money in your hand and go to the place which the Lord your God chooses. And you may spend the money for whatever your heart desires, for oxen, or sheep, or wine, or strong drink, or whatever your heart desires; and there you shall eat in the presence of the Lord your God and rejoice, you and your household (Deuteronomy 14:22-26).

• Tithe given to support Levites and poor To the sons of Levi, behold, I have given all the tithe in Israel for an inheritance, in return for their service which they perform, the service of the tent of meeting... the tithe of the sons of Israel, which they offer as an offering to the Lord, I have given to the Levites (Numbers 18:21-24). At the end of every third year you shall bring out all the tithe of your produce in that year, and shall deposit it in your town. And the Levite, because he has no portion or inheritance among you, and the alien, the orphan and the widow who are in your town, shall come and eat and be satisfied (Deuteronomy 14:28-29).

When you have finished paying all the tithe of your increase in the third year, the year of tithing, then you shall give it to the Levite, to the stranger, to the orphan and to the widow, that they may eat in your towns, and be satisfied (Deuteronomy 26:12). Also he commanded the people who lived in Jerusalem to give the portion due to the priests and the Levites, that they might devote themselves to the law of the Lord. And as soon as the order spread, the sons of Israel... brought in abundantly the tithe of all. And the sons of Israel and Judah who lived in the cities of Judah, also brought in the tithe of oxen and sheep, and the tithe of sacred gifts which were consecrated to the Lord their God... Since the contributions began to be brought into the house of the Lord, we have had enough to eat with plenty left over, for the Lord has blessed His people, and this great quantity is left over... they faithfully brought in the contributions and the tithes (2 Chronicles 31:4-12).

We will also bring... the tithe of our ground to the Levites, for the Levites are they who receive the tithes in all the rural towns. And the priest, the son of Aaron, shall be with the Levites when the Levites receive tithes (Nehemiah 10:37-38). I also discovered that the portions of the Levites had not been given them, so that the Levites and the singers who performed the service had gone away, each to his own field. So I reprimanded the officials and said, "Why is the house of God forsaken?" (Nehemiah 13:10-11).

• Levites were to tithe from their tithe Moreover, you shall speak to the Levites and say to them, 'When you take from the sons of Israel the tithe... then you shall present an offering from it to the Lord, a tithe of the tithe (Numbers 18:26).

3. Tithe in the New Testament

• Jesus condemns the Pharisees

• The superiority of priesthood of Melchizedek Melchizedek, king of Salem, priest of the Most High God, who met Abraham as he was returning from the slaughter of the kings and blessed him, to whom also Abraham apportioned a tenth part of all the spoils...observe how great this man was to whom Abraham, the patriarch, gave a tenth of the choicest spoils. And those indeed of the sons of Levi who receive the priest's office have commandment in the Law to collect a tenth from the people, that is, from their brethren, although these are descended from Abraham. But the one whose genealogy is not traced from them collected a tenth from Abraham, and blessed the one who had the promises. But without any dispute the lesser is blessed by the greater. And in this case mortal men receive tithes, but in that case one receives them, of whom it is witnessed that he lives on. And, so to speak, through Abraham even Levi, who received tithes, paid tithes (Hebrews 7:1-2, 4-9).

4. Storehouse tithe Then Hezekiah commanded them to prepare rooms in the house of the Lord, and they prepared them. And they faithfully brought in the contributions and the tithes (2 Chronicles 31:11-12). The Levites shall bring up the tenth of the tithes to the house of our God, to the storehouse (Nehemiah 10:38). On that day men were also appointed over the chambers for the stores, the contributions, the first fruits, and the tithes (Nehemiah 12:44). All Judah then brought the tithe of the grain, wine, and oil into the storehouses (Nehemiah 13:12).

B. OFFERINGS

C. PROPORTIONATE GIVING (AS GOD PROSPERS) Then you shall celebrate the Feast of Weeks to the Lord your God with a tribute of a freewill offering of your hand, which you shall give just as the Lord your God blesses you... Every man shall give as he is able, according to the blessing of the Lord your God which He has given you (Deuteronomy 16:10, 16). Each one of you put aside and save, as he may prosper, that no collections be made I come (1 Corinthians 16:2).

1. Examples of proportionate giving According to their ability they gave to the treasury for the work (Ezra 2:69). In the proportion that any of the disciples had means, each of them determined to send a contribution (Acts 11:29). 2. Acceptable amount given in proportion to one's means For if the readiness is

present [to give], it is acceptable according to what a man has, not according to what he does not have (2 Corinthians 8:12)

D. SACRIFICIAL GIVING

He sat down opposite the treasury, and began observing how the multitude were putting money into the treasury; and many rich people were putting in large sums. And a poor widow came and put in two small copper coins, which amount to a cent. And calling His disciples to Him, He said to them, "Truly I say to you, this poor widow put in more than all the contributors to the treasury; for they all put in out of their surplus, but she, out of poverty, put in all she owned, all she had to live on" (Mark 12:41-44). He looked up and saw the rich putting their gifts into the treasury. And He saw a certain poor widow putting in two small copper coins. And He said, "Truly I say to you, this poor widow put in more than all of them; for they all out of their surplus put into the offering; but she out of her poverty put in all that she had to live on" (Luke 21:1-4). Now, brethren, we wish to make known to you the grace of God which has been given in the churches of Macedonia, that in a great ordeal of affliction their abundance of joy and their deep poverty overflowed in the wealth of their liberality. For I testify that according to their ability, and beyond their ability they gave of their own accord, begging us with much entreaty for the favor of participation in the support of the saints (2 Corinthians 8:1-4).

1. Do not give something that costs you nothing "Why has my lord the king come to his servant? And David said, "To buy the threshing floor from you, in order to build an altar to the Lord, that the plague may be held back from the people." And Araunah said to David, "Let my lord the king take and offer ...the king said to Araunah, "No, but I will surely buy it from you for a price, for I will not offer burnt offerings to the Lord my God which cost me nothing (2 Samuel 24:21-24). David said to Ornan, "Give me the site of this threshing floor, that I may build on it an altar to the Lord; for the full price you shall give it to me, that the plague may be restrained from the people." And

Ornan said to David, "Take it for yourself... David said to Ornan, "No, but I will surely buy it for the full price; for I will not take what is yours for the Lord, or offer a burnt offering which costs me nothing" (1 Chronicles 21:22-24).

2. Cursed when giving something stolen or blemished When you present the blind for sacrifice, is it not evil? And when you present the lame and sick, is it not evil?... With such an offering on your part, will He receive any of you kindly?" says the Lord of hosts... you bring what was taken by robbery, and what is lame or sick; so you bring the offering! Should I receive that from your hand?" says the Lord. "But cursed be the swindler who has a male in his flock, and vows it, but sacrifices a blemished animal to the Lord, for I am a great King," says the Lord of hosts, "and My name is feared among the nations" (Malachi 1:6-14).

www.ingramcontent.com/pod-product-compliance
Lightning Source LLC
Chambersburg PA
CBHW071332190426
43193CB00041B/1747